The Cluttered Mind of

Aneri Yendis

ANERI YENDIS

The Cluttered Mind of Aneri Yendis

(Your mind's playing tricks on you). Is an understatement when feelings and thoughts are compressed and concealed. Words that need to be spoken, fester and mold into hard, callus, negative emotions. Thoughts consume your mind and take up precious grooves and canals. To contain these fatal thoughts, walls are built around them, not to infect other parts of your brain. Feelings of fear, betrayal, injustice, anger and loneliness. Turning good days into bad ones.

The Cluttered Mind of Aneri Yendis, is a collection of traditional poems to promote conversation and discussion. Unpretentious an intentionally simplistic in nature, to ignite dialogue on race, religion and culture.

Aneri Yendis, routinely passive and subdued. Shares her inner emotions and concealed sentiments. That can be relevant to all communities.

Poems re-counting, growing up in a small predominantly white town, relationships, childbirth and illness.

The poems in this book – express the frustration, fear and loneliness she and others had/must face daily. A window into the mind and heart of black women in their communities and the world.

Utilizing poetry as a vehicle to express her compressed thoughts and feelings. To help unclutter the words, emotions and break down walls in the mind of Aneri Yendis.

Black Lives

Black America (ins) continue to contribute, influence and impact America's culture and the world. The history of our interwoven uniqueness and heritage. Puts an exclamation mark next to our legacy.

America's views of reparation for slavery.
A never-ending cycle of "I didn't do it"
and "get over it" conveyed by the government
and White America.

Going to school in a small white town.
The progress and advantages of being

raised in that environment,

come with its own problems.

Honoring the beauty of black.

Colorism is rampant in the entertainment industry.

Which conveys the message to the world "bright is right"

A shout out to the paper bag

brothers and sisters!

Thank You Our Kings

To all the black men who stand tall.

They chose to stay with black women an

breakdown those walls.

Rose above the stereotypes and societies lies.

They are, black woman's true love an ultimate prize.

They are the true heroes to our babies.

They always walk in GOD's light.

Answer is always yes, never no, or maybe.

Puts his family first does whatever it takes.

Works two jobs – whatever

till his body aches.

Uses his mind more than his mouth.

The number of strong black Kings stretch from

North to South.

From a Queen to her King,

Thank you, my love.

I'm always by your side,

and in awe of.

150 Years Ago

It happened 150 years ago
Black people need to let it go.

Yeah you picked cotton and sugar cane
we stole you from your continent and
stripped you of your name.

Some of you yes, were whipped
some women yes, were raped.
Yes, some of you were hanged
when you tried to escape.

But it's time to move on, stop talking about
America's sin.
It's time to just accept it, bare it
and grin.
Yes, thank you for your sweat and blood to build this
rich, great country.
Yes, you did it for free and didn't get any
money.

No recognition or parades
buried in shallow unmarked
graves.
Children ripped from their mother's
arms.
Fathers sold to work on other farms.
Yes, your heritage and pride stripped.
language and religion

replaced.
Many killed themselves before
their identities were erased.

So, you're talking again about reparations
for what was done to you.
Why can't you be like the
Apache and Sioux?
We killed them also
took their land.
Moved them to unwanted parts of
the country to do their
Rain dance.
Be like the Asians and sit quietly
and cook your rice.
Show us respect and smile and
be nice.
They know how to act and
stay in their lane.
Make the best of their lives and the
best Chow Mein.
There will never be reparations
we have apologized enough.
If you push the issue, there will be
more of you in handcuffs.
You had a black president
you're allowed to vote.
Don't blame us, we won't
be your scapegoat.
We don't own slaves
most of us aren't rich.
You blacks have a nerve

You sons of a bitch.

You came for a "shit hole"

my president said.

You should thank GOD for slavery

your continent is full of bloodshed.

Yes, Jim Crow was wrong

burning churches wasn't GOD like.

Destroying black villages, killing innocent

black people like the

Third Reich.

Killing innocent children

jailing innocent men.

To keep legal slavery going

signing away freedom with a

fountain pen.

Yes, you fought in every war

this country has faced.

Your patriotism and honor often

erased.

The contributions are numerous

reparations would

break the banks.

So, it will never happen

just accept our

Thanks.

Thanks for soul, country, rock & roll music

stop lights, paper bags, peanut butter

and other uses.

Just know that we know what 'you

have done for this country.

Don't get mad or offended if

someone calls you a

monkey.

Yes, cops kill innocent people

just by the color of their skin.

Yes, some white parents teach

racism and prejudice before

their child's life begins.

Yes, black lives matter

just not as much as mine.

Even though we share a common history

and even a bloodline.

Freedom for all is what we teach

but freedom for all – all won't

reach.

Enjoy your black history month

enjoy your MLK day.

There will never be

REPARATIONS

that's all we have to say......

Decedents of Uncle Sam

Black women's heartache

The lies told to black women to keep them in their place
the lies told to black women was a disgrace.

You must be strong for black men,
they are under a lot of pressure.
The "MAN" is after him.
More than you can measure.

You belong to black men,
NO - one other.
Don't be mad if he lays down,
with a different color.

One day he will return back
to black women.
He just needs to have fun.
Take care of the black community,
take care of everyone.

Let him sow his oats,
play his games.
While you work and
become a scholar.
He will admire your strength your success.
Don't mind if he lives in squalor.
It's your job to take care of him now,
he's home after 20 years of play.
Give him a chance, hear him out
please let him stay.

Coming from an old, broke black man,

who let a black woman hold the line.

We should have known better

should have known you were our gold mine.

Everything we needed could be found in you,

Our grandmothers' mother's auntie's and sisters

were the strongest crew.

You raised our kids without our help

to grow and do better.

Some went down our same path,

I see them in the homeless shelter.

I tried to tell them to get it together,

and to behave,

Their heart is so far broken

the next place is the grave.

I'm sorry to all my black Queens

my mom, my sisters especially my baby girls

a black man's debt to black women can't be paid

with diamonds and pearls.

Only with our life of change and putting the black family

First.

Colors of Black

Deep Midnight black
Your eyes drown within the hue.
The closet resemblance of GOD.
Your color is strength…purity…and true.
Mahogany
The color of our continent
Africa
The color of earth and soil.
Your tone the true color
of our pharaoh's kings and queens
African royal.

Cinnamon/ Brown Sugar
The color of sweetness and spice.
The mixture of shame – betrayal -and malice
the color of the ultimate
Sacrifice.
All the colors of black across
a multitude of continents.
Doesn't take away from our
African roots.
Or, say that we lack.
Our different shades and
different tongues shouts
"Black is Black!"

Black culture

Black is not a fashion statement
a lipstick or perfume.
It's not a role you stop and go
put down an reassume.
Black is not a hip-hop rap
jingle or R&B song.
It's not an after-school program
Or a clique to belong.
Black is not a fad,
stage you're going through
or a trend.
Black is not a half and half
what am I
straddling friend.
Black is strength pride
an endurance.
Black is truth and love
despite our circumstance.
Black is hope survival
and a profound history.
Black is standing tall
and shouting "victory".
So, all the people with shades of black
who feel they don't belong?
Don't bring up my leaders
call on Ponce DeLeon.
Don't call out
Martin Luther King

Malcolm X

or Rosa Parks.

Our culture is our history,

our trademarks.

So, when prejudice and discrimination

slap you in the face.

Remember you're not black

you are some other type of race.

Hate to be Black... Sometimes

Sometimes I just don't want to be black,
cause black can be stupid,
Crazy, and drawback.
Some don't speak when you say "hi,"
look at you crazy and you ask yourself why?
Buy clothes and cars we can't afford.
Ducking in dodging Rent-a-Center and the landlord.
Name our kids weird ass names
like Beautify, Bonquisha,
Koolaidorea and Topramenisha.
Becoming a life coach
after getting out of jail.
Then get arrested for
scamming people's email.
Black men are dating
everything but black.
Black women going crazy
living off a coffee and Prozac.
One out of Three are
Bi, trans gender or just gay.
Fighting videos on Facebook
on some hearsay.
Church is full of demon pastors
preying on money.
God like on Sabbath day.
Devils on Monday.
Children have lost all respect
for their elders.

Forgot about the price that was paid

by their ancestors.

Women shouting, "I love to be black".

Wearing fake everything

and blonde hair to their crack.

Yes, there are black people

who have blue eyes and blonde hair.

Their hair is curly like cotton

not flowing in the air

Well, I guess black

like everything else has lost its quality.

The unknowing price we paid

for equality.

Nappy Hair

Kinky, curly, frizzy or straight
It's my hair not yours,
just sit there and hate.
Whether head grown or brought from the store.
Once it's on my head it's mine to adore.
All hair is good hair one inch of it or a mile.
No matter how I work it, color it, braided my style.
So, to all the stupid black men, with stupid
comments about black women's air.
We really don't care.
Because we know, your toupee can't compare.

Opportunity

Two homeless men, both without a job

one white, one black sit on a park bench every day watching the world, like an angry mob.

Sneering and swearing feeling sorry for themselves bathing in self-pity drowning in sorry full wells.

One day a local deli owner approaches the first and says, "I have an opportunity to offer you. To open the deli, my wife is ill. To put out the tables and chairs napkins to refill. I have a small apartment in the back for you, some money in your pocket a dollar or two. The white man jumps up and says, "yes that will do". Leaving the black man on the bench alone wondering (why not me too).

For a couple of months, the white man does his job but slowly starts sleeping late, once again becoming a slob. The deli owner finally tells him it's time to leave. He's once again on that park bench. A sight that's hard to believe.

A week or two goes by and the black man gets up from the bench. He walks across the street to the deli owner and says without a flinch. "I overheard the opportunity you offered my friend; I would like that same opportunity with a slight mend. In addition to the tasks you required for him to do. I will do other tasks that a suitable for you". The deli owner agreed to give him a chance but warned him he will boot him out without a second glance.

The black man moved in and does his work. Goes from a janitor to the best deli clerk. From deli clerk to assistant manager, finally gets his own place. Becomes pride of the deli family, accomplishments put on showcase.

The white man one day sees the black man drive by. Looks at the black man and ask "what?" "how?" "why?" Oh, affirmative action, that's it he took my job, he has my life. Looking around acknowledging his life is full of strife. Yells and screams how that black man stole my opportunity. Believing his white skin gives him some type

of immunity. Immunity to hard work, dedication and knowledge. Drinking, smoking, acting a fool forgoing college. White privilege can take you only so far. The rest you must do to get the gold and caviar.

The black man must do twice as much to get the same prize. He worked harder and smarter. Because he realized. Being black in America, you must prove your worth first. White people have worth straight from birth.

Small White Town

Four black kids on a bus
sitting very still.
Four black kids on a bus
no one knows how it feels.
"Why can't your hair move? Why does it feel like that? I didn't
know black people lived here. Where do you live at?"
"Why do black people steal? Why do they kill? My daddy
said-all are bad and can't pay their bills"
"We hate nigger music" we have to hear this every day. Some
white kids trying to act tough to make us go away.
Four black kids on a bus- before we start to scream. In our
minds, we repeat this couldn't be Doctor King's Dream.

Where is Black

Where is the color black?
I can't find it in the box
122 colors and no black
"What the fox?"
The little white girl
used it to make her hair black
like mine.
The little brown boy used it
to make his car black and shine.
I guess my picture will be
invisible to see.
Just like how the world see's
black people,

Like Me.

Why

Why can't real ice cream and chips be on
Keto?
Why can't I eat all the candy I want?
And still be slim and neat o?

Why does celery and carrots
Taste so bland?
Why can't I blame my weight gain,
on my thyroid gland?

Why does sugar and corn syrup
cause diabetes?
Whole grain, skim milk is
not on my list of treaties.

I want to eat Twizzlers, Now & Laters
Skittles and chips.
And still not gain weight on
my face, arms and hips.

Eat pancakes with real syrup
and fries till I puke.
No spinach, kale, and
almond milk, I rebuke.

Well, until fat white woman
become the standard of beauty.
No one will admire
my big fat black
bootie.

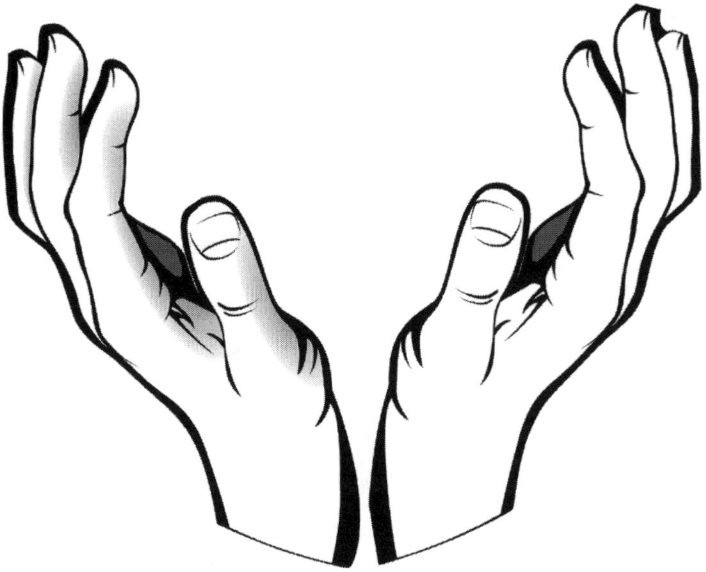

Faith

Testimony of GOD's love for me.
Acknowledging and believing he lives in me,
and anyone who accepts him.

People's perception of dialysis patients.

Never being able to hide from death
he will always find you.

Kidney Disease

1 Liter

Water the nectar of the God's is what I have been told. Is cold crisp going down, to quench your very soul.

Over ice - in hot tea - Kool-aid or snow cone. On a hot summer day or winter that chills to the bone.

But what if you can't drink water, or just a little bit. Because your kidneys aren't working right and your doctor said 1 liter, that's it.

Water that is free and comes out the tap. Could kill you by drowning, before you could even snap. The cruel irony is; the one thing that is free. You can not have, because your body can't make pee.

Blood

I saw my blood today spinning inside a machine. Gears turning it around and around getting it nice and clean.

My kidneys aren't working right so I do these 3 times a week. If this doesn't get done. My future is less than bleak.

I have met so many people like me some young and not so old. They all have a story to tell and felt good once is was told. We all want people to respect us not pity our trials and pain. Don't dismiss our concerns or say we're to blame.

Don't whisper, stare, taunt or put on a fur surd. Because like they say, "Only by the grace of God".

Can't Hide

Knock… Knock open the door
it's time to let me in!
Knock… Knock open the door
don't let me say it again!

Hey There! Open the door-
you can hide from me
NEVER!
Your family and friends' prayers,
won't last forever.

I am DEATH and I answer all calls

So, you won't open the door

OH Look!
is that a crack in the
WALL?

Prideful Thoughts

I thought I'll have a mass of wealth set like a king. To
impress you with all with jewels gold and bling.

I thought I'd have a slim trim body to impress you with style. To have
high fashion, shoes pocketbooks and accessories for miles.

I thought I'd have two degrees to impress you with my scholar. To
work in an office and be considered cooperate white collar.

I only have a little house one thousand debt or under. I only have a
P.H.D. public high school diploma. I only have a running van, no
payments or thrills. No high insurance payments no extra bills. No
Jaguar, no BMW or Escalade. Just good old Plymouth – USA made.

I hope you can forgive my prideful thoughts. I miss seeing you all. I avoided
you my family, I avoided even your call. I want to see my brothers and kiss
them everyday. I want to remember when we use to play. I want to see my
relatives today. My pride kept me from seeing my grandma I miss you Tere-
tha Ma. I miss my aunt Alberta her husband James as well. This people
shaped and molded my life and I stayed away because I didn't excel.
Please forgive me for all my prideful thoughts I thought I needed to
impress. I now know I needed love oh how I have been blessed.

They prayed for me they prayed for me when my kidneys made me ill. I hadn't
seen some of them in over twenty years. But they still did God's will.

Forgive me.

Strong

I am strong – I will fight this
I have the power of Prayer.
I have the armor of the Lord and he stands before me.

I am strong- I will win this
I have the power of family. The strength of numbers holding a line will defeat all battles.

I am strong- I will conquer this disease and stand strong and tall.
I have the belief of victory in my heart and soul and I know I won't be wrong.

I am strong- my body may be weak now.
But fighting the fight of my life will make me
STRONG

Heavenly Anointed

"Girl you been touched by God"

My cup hath runneth over,
my world had a friendly takeover.

God walks with me
and, carries me a lot.
The bond we have is tighter then,
a love knot.

Forgave me for my choices and,
dropping his hand.
Quickly grabbing me up
when sinking in quicksand.
Washed me again,
a million times.
So clean again, my heart chimes.

The devil knows I'm a favorite child.
He always sends his demons,
the one with the cutest smiles.

I tried to be strong, but they know
my weakness.
But I always call out
"Help me Jesus".

He fights my illness and,
my enemies.

He is; my all-in-one remedies.

So, when someone says
"Girl you been touched by God".
I look at the heavens,
and watch the Angels applaud.

Thank you
Heavenly Father

What if it's not real?

What if it's all not real? Just a wonderful book. What if it's
all made believe? So, don't give it another look.

No Heaven...No Hell no paradise. Just play your cards and like the roll of the
dice. So, go to work go to play. If you wake up tomorrow for another day. It was
just by chance; your heart still beats. No higher power. No heavenly feat.

No Living God. No son of man. No Holy Spirit. No everlasting hand. No
sacrifice. No washed as snow. No holes in hand. No better place to go.

My life is proof that its all real. Born three months early had to stay in a plas-
tic seal. Four operations emotional relationships, a black eye and two busted lips.
Welfare shelter two kids out of wedlock. No food, no money living on Hell's block.

Raped in college, abandoned by my kid's dad. Miles from my family no support from
the friends I had. Got a call from the doctor saying your kidneys are failing fast. Get
to ER or your life won't last. I should have been gone already my numbers were off
the chart. My heart should have stopped beating. And this world I would depart.

Something held me here. Someone held my hand. Someone carried me
across that troubled sand. I know it is my Loving Lord. I know that he
is REAL. I know every time I take a breath. His spirit is revealed.

So, this is my testament to the world that I serve a Living God. I
thank him for all my troubles, because I know if I walked alone. I
wouldn't have made it. I'm here because he lives in me.

Two Weeks Each Summer

The first two weeks in July we drive down to see our family. We
pack our car, grab our pillows and set out to join our history.

We live so far from our clan, our people, folks or kin. We can
only see them two weeks when the summers begin.

We drive to Virginia and go to 220 South, to see grandma, Joyce and
the crew. We have so many people like Alex, Terry to name a few.
We bar-b-que drink iced tea, swim in the public pool. Learn
the new dances, hair styles and how to be cool.

The next year we drive to Belton to see Alberta and James. See all the
kids and chickens. Play farmyard country games. We pick fresh straw-
berries eat sugar stalk. Lay under the stars and talk...talk...talk.
We then go the church on Sunday to sang, rejoice and shout. Go home
eat fried chicken, corn on the cob and spit watermelon seeds out.

Its time to go back North where slaves ran to be free. Its time
to cross that line where happiness is no longer the key.
Thank you forever my
Lord.
The Cluttered Mind of Aneri Yendis

Family

Self

No one is born with

Self - esteem

Self - confidence

Self - worth

these things you learn and felt at birth.

You learn in how you are loved.

How you are respected.

How you are hugged and kissed.

How you are protected.

If you doubt the child - self, you will doubt the adult -self.

So, parents teach your child

Self -esteem

Self – confidence

Self - worth

So, they will grow wise and strong prosperous on this earth.

Spare the rod

Don't spank – Don't yell
no timeout
no discipline.

Just talk calmly
and softly
to your children.
Spare the rod
let them learn
on their own.
It's not good
to make them
cry and moan.
Let child services
diagnose them with
a three- or four-letter code.
Put a price tag
on them
and a barcode.
Have them talk to a therapist,
and make you pay
the bills.
Have your children
taking handfuls
of pills.
We have become a nation
of pill pushers. Because we turned away from
GOD.

We stopped following

his law

"Don't spare the Rod"

Foolish Child

You, foolish child-you, foolish child
You wasted so much time.
You hated her for so long for things
Done long ago.

She lied to me!
She left me!
She pushed me away!

You, foolish child-you, foolish child
you wasted so much time.

She lied to cover shame and pain.
She left to make a better life.
She pushed you hard to be better than her.

You, foolish child-you, foolish child
You wasted so much time.

She is here brushing my hair.
She is here washing my face.
She is here holding my hand- hearing I may die.
She has always been here- waiting for me to Stop being a

Foolish Child.

Little Sister

My first child I had when I was twelve my little sister came to me and changed my world. I feed her milk and changed her pants and watched her sleep so sound. I made her cry with a song and laugh with a frown.

I got tired of her-when I was sixteen and left her on the side. Got mad when I had to play with her seek and hide. She's not my child so why I have to do this crap and make me wear this hat. It's bad enough to share a room with this little brat.

I left home at eighteen and came home once a year. I turned around one day, and she wasn't there. She had left to start her life to learn and spread her wings. I miss those simple times and simple things. I wish I talked more and put her on my back. Carried her around and didn't give any slack.

She is the crowning jewel of our clan she travels the world with knowledge in hand. Educator-mentor businesswoman of conviction. Purpose-poise-substance Commentator of submission.

My little sister I'm so proud of all your worth and goal. To know I may have played a minor part as a big sister in my role.

Miracle

I fell in love today
A miracle was revealed. I waited months and months
for my love.
My joy couldn't be concealed.

Another boy I was carrying. Three ultrasounds
confirmed.
Jacobi would be his name,
our love was
re-affirmed.

It's a girl! It's girl!
I was told coming out of my sleep.
"A girl"? "A girl"? I questioned falling
back asleep.

"A girl"! I screamed finally awake
understanding what I was told.
The tears fell, my body shock
I couldn't self – control.

I fell to my knees and thanked my GOD
he heard my silent prayer.
I prayed for a little girl like me
to declare my heir.
She was and IS my miracle,
my angel
on this earth.
A grown woman now, on her own
but I will never forget her
birth.

Voices

Small little faces staring out the window.
Looking for yesterday.
Not caring about today.
Doubting tomorrow.
Screaming in their heads
"I want to go home!".
Ceasing to exist in their heart.
"I don't want to play!
Where is my mommy"?
"Mommy?" "Mommy"?
"No"!
"I don't want to play!"
"Where is my mom"?
"Mom"! "Mom"!
"I'm not playing!"
"Leave me alone"!
"Ma". "Ma".

"Yeah I'll play".
"Fuck her".

You Told Me So

"You told me so"
do you think that's what I want to hear?
"You told me so"
that's why I don't come near.
I don't come home but once in a while.
Cause, "I told you so", is concealed by a smile.
You don't think I know I messed up my life.
I haven't thought about ending it all with a
kitchen knife.
Yes, I have but the reason I stay.
Is because of those two kids,
the one you told me to throw away.
They are my mission to go on living.
To be strong for them and always forgiving.
"Yes,
you told me so".
OK; there it is.
Did you listen to your mother?
Answer that quiz.

My Dad

Oh, my dad... Oh, my dad
Where do I begin?
A man who's quiet at times showed his love from within.
He never talked on the phone just handed it to my mom.
But just hearing the words "Hey Baby" was all your heart would long.
He works so hard-and so long he wasn't always there.
But you know he did it all for you and all the one's he care.
I found out at 30 he really wasn't mine. But I grew
up saying we have the same nose
Oh, how I was so blind.
We don't have the same nose-but the same heart, mind and soul
He chose to be my dad and to carry the toll.
To raise a child that wasn't his- to give her his last name.
To make that child his life and love
Oh, where do I begin?

My Last Goodbye

Why does this hurt so much?
I knew the time would come
To hear the words "I'm moving out"
I never thought to hear it from this one.

She slept with me until she was five
And cried everyday I left for work
She hated going to school and, on the corner, she would lurk

The first one already left, and my heart was breaking with shame
He left to live in a cold hard world with no Knowl-
edge-money or God's word to claim

When she leaves- my heart will be cold
Because I will lose my child
All my feelings of fear and loneliness will begin to run wild

I beg my Lord to fill that void to hold
And tame me
To lose my child-my best friend-my love-
My Jamie

My Son

I can't believe he's finally here ten fingers and toes —and all that hair.
32 hours of labor and all that strain
C-section and blood with all that pain.
Breastfeeding and crying throughout the night. Dirty
dishes boiled bottles-no rest in sight.

Now 21 years old and on his own. A little boy of his own to make him groan. To
hustle and scratch to make away. To deal with baby mamma drama everyday.

He came over yesterday to say I miss you. To say he was sorry for how
he dissed me to. He missed my love-he missed my home- my cook-
ing and my smile. He knows how hard it is- he has walked a mile.

Then the doorbell rang, and I awoke. It was my son at the door saying he was
broke. Could he get ten dollars until payday? I promise to pay you back.

Yea… Yea right O.K.

I Love you my baby boy!!!!!!

Relationships

Relationships are a balancing act between two people. Each trying to stand their own ground and carry themselves and each other.

Protesters outside women clinics.
The right to free speech and demonstration,
carries a distorted concept of one's truth.

Betrayal, fear and masking the truth.
That reshaped my entrance to womanhood.

Not being played,
or bullied into doing something,
you don't want to do.

Relationship is not a fairy tale.

Playing house

Falling in love is easy.
Staying in love takes
Work.
hard work
dedicated work
commitment work
trust work
loyalty work
GOD's work
communication work
faith work
pleasure work
peace work
sharing work
laughter work
emotional work
If you're not ready to put in work
don't play - house.

My Choice

They stand outside the women's clinic
with signs of discontent.

Not knowing the emotions of
guilt, shame and betrayal
those messages are meant.

Don't judge me or my
choice to choose.
Don't shame me to relinquish
my right.

Don't tell me It's
GOD's decision
And the choice I make
I can't rewrite.

My choice to walk in the light
doesn't mean there isn't
any gray.
My life is full of color,
not just black and white
on any day.

GOD made me a descendent of
Eve.
To be strong and true
to accept decisions, I make
and seek his help,

no approval needed from

You.

I don't have to explain myself

my body is mine.

My womb belongs to me.

The sperm that fertilized this egg

by chance.

Could have easily went

"Skee...Skee...Skee."

Fat Ass

Oh, you have such a pretty face
but don't you know the rest is a disgrace.
Fat on your neck
fat on your arms
fat on your back and trunk
fat legs, hands, feet and nothing cute with that junk.
Your eyes are an A
so why can't you see.
The rest of your body makes you a D.
Your lips are so soft, round and pout,
but who wants to kiss someone short, fat and stout?

Is being fat oh so bad- I ask myself each day
I raise my kids – go to work but still I have to say.

My fat ass brought houses- my fat ass had two kids
My fat ass pays taxes- so tell me what gives.
If being fat is such a curse or shame to bring
I know a lot of skinny people-who don't have a thing.

So, kiss my fat ass!!

Don't ask me for Shit

Don't ask me for shit,
you man born bitch.

I work hard to keep us straight,
but you always walk away and can't communicate.

Boast and brag about the shit I brought.
But the money I spent,
is an afterthought.

My VCR my pots and pans.
My kids, my future plans.

It's sad I wasted so many years,
looking back at all the pain and tears.

The line is drawn in the sand,
you should've been born
with a pussy.
'cause you're not a man.
Me and my kids are out.
WE FIRST!

Flower's in Hand

No…Stop! I'm not ready for this. This is so not cool.

No… Stop! I'm not ready for this. We should be back at school.

No… Stop! I'm not ready for this. Can't you hear me scream?

No… Stop! I'm not ready for this. This is not how it happens in my dream.

Where are the candles? Where is the music? Where are the flowers in hand? Where is the blanket on the beach? Wine glasses in the sand.

You're taking my womanhood you're taking my pride. My prize I hold so dear. You're taking my identity you're taking myself and leaving me with just fear.

AHHH!!!!you took away my promise to God you stripped it before my eyes. You took my vow to myself based on little lies.

"What are you crying about your eighteen and in college? It's time to have fun, play it's not all about the knowledge"

What happens between us, don't make such a fuss. I'm your boyfriend "your man" giving up the booty is a must.

I felt so lost so all alone nowhere to talk or turn. So, I told myself to forget it and next time I will learn.

I made up a story about my first a tall handsome soldier man. Who swept me off my feet with candy, sunsets and flowers in hand.

The Price of Love

They say you can't buy love,
love comes free.
Not in the hood - take it from me.
Newport's and a 40
can buy you a man.
Chronic and Gin
he's in your Afghan.
Pork rinds and chips
he is kissing your lips.
Jordan's and Kobe's
he will be your young trophies.
Love is a 4-letter word that
some will get with, luck
the rest of us will
settle for buying a
F**k.

How dare you!!!

I gave it to who? What did you say?

And even if I did. I don't have to throw it your way.

My pussy is mine and something I don't toss around

I don't care what he said. Touch me again, I will knock you to the ground.

Oh, I shouldn't worry, you can't have kids.

You were stung by a spider, so your sperm is rid.

You must think I'm a fool, or you are just to cool

My womanhood is my prize, my bond to God

My jewel.

Turning back time

If I knew what I know now - back, then
would I make the same mistakes again?

Love a man who only loved himself
or put all the love in me, build up oneself.

Educate my mind keep the knowledge going
or be afraid to try, always unknowing.

Keep the little seed I threw away
or make my choice and fill my heart decay.

We can never turn back time or change the past
just live with our mistakes and be steadfast.

Our mistakes shape us and prepare us for the battles of life.
But you must forgive yourself
FIRST!